BRAVE ON THE ROCKS

IF YOU DON'T GO,
you don't see

SABRINA WARD HARRISON

foreword by Hilary Swank

Villard (V) NEW YORK

Also by Sabrina Ward Harrison

Spilling Open: The Art of Becoming Yourself

FOR MOLLY

POPPY

DEDICATED TO THE MEMORY OF
HER MOTHER, JAN FRANKS,

HER LOVE AND LAUGHTER
FILLS THE SPACE BETWEEN US.

A Token of Affection.

FOREWORD

*"I've been consumed with all this living up to something, to 'be something,' 'express something'!
We have such a longing to be understood and loved by the other. Why? Can't it be just this now?
Without the armor and shields, just myself? My vulnerability protects me, not my tight control.
I hope to love with an open hand and a slow trusting stride."*

—SPILLING OPEN

I first came across Sabrina Ward Harrison's art and writing while flipping through a magazine on a
plane last summer. I was drawn in by her candid sincerity and willingness to be so open with her feelings and thoughts.

I feel more than honored to offer my appreciation for Sabrina's work by writing this opening to
Brave on the Rocks. In the continuum of life and trying to discover my true self, Sabrina reminds
me, through her brave, insightful, and heartfelt honesty, that we are all connected in this journey.
We are connected through an intertwining sameness called the struggles and joys of finding and
becoming our authentic selves. When I read her words, I felt acknowledged for my journey and for
being a woman in these complex times. There are not adequate words to fully express my thank-
fulness for having found Sabrina. Thank you, Sabrina, for sharing your gift with us. May we all con-
tinue to share our journeys together so we know we are not alone.

Thank you, thank you, thank you!

Peace and love,
Hilary Swank, actor

What

what A few years this has been!

* The decision TO PUBLISH
your OWN private growing-up journal—
while you're still growing up—is an
An interesting one.
(it is called Spilling Open: THE ART OF BECOMING YOURSELF)

yikes. yes. yup i did this in 1999.

The Response has been amazing.
Ultimately I feel I could HAVE\WOULD HAVE
Lived my life never realizing HOW MANY OTHERS
FEEL THESE Questions and feelings like MYSELF.
I did not know this at all
I felt I might be so crazy to do this and
WHEN I WAS PUBLISHING IT—
PEOPLE WOULD JUST LAUGH at me and at Spilling Open
I HAD TO Let those ego-voices go and trust
THAT just writing it DOWN frees it from

being stuck inside. If one other person could
breathe a little EASIER FROM me sharing some of my
life in progress then I MUST SHARE IT.

——————→ But NOW.... where are my limits?

Because I have SHARED this MUCH—
should I SHARE MORE?

DO I HAVE TO?
will it help me?
what is just mine?

I THINK what HAS BEEN an ODD part of THIS success

I THINK what HAS also Been an ODD thing about this experience of ~~Spilling~~ publishing Spilling OPEN is that growing UP I've never felt very good at anything. NOT being an athlete, academic OR CHEERLEADER IN HIgh school Left me sorta wandering, in Low expectations of Myself.

BEING actually recognized FOR being an "author" now OR "PUBLISHED"... was so different and amazingly RANDOM to Me.

Suddenly, I was PUSHING MYSEIf SO HARD to Live up to this feeling LikE "Well IF THESE GUYS See something good, valuable in ME, I better NOT Let these readers DOWN!"

IT WAS THESE TIMES I HAD TO TURN TO Spilling OPEN AND Remind myself again of what the real messages are in the BOOK——IF I encourage OTHERS to feel how they Really Feel, to BE FORGIVING OF the contradictions, then I must turn this TOWARDS Myself. I AM NOT A ~~Finished~~ PRODUCT.

Finished

THE decision to travel to Italy alone
was a huge turning POINt in my Life.
I HAD Nothing Left in me to give — But to
GIVE SOMETHING Lost BACK TO MY SELF. and so with my
$550.00 ticket + A BackPack I Left.
       AS I HAVE MADE   BRAVE ON THE ROCKS   I have
HAD Flashes of "OH come on SABrina this isnt BOLD
enough, it isnt Africa OR the Peace Corps"
   But I remind MYself — of those SAME Feelings I
HAD Before Publishing SPILLing OPEN — "My life
is so Ordinary WHO wants to read this?"
       BUT NOW I feel WE NEED MORE BOOKS
BY us "Ordinary FOLKS" just Making our
WAY through our Lives. We need
that connectiON. TO kNOW WE are not aLone.
     our Questions are necessary.

Over and Over again I am touched ~~by~~ and Blessed By the readers WHO tell ME THAT Spilling OPEN has in some way Helped them to feel a little less alone a little more okay being messy, and a little MORE Brave. I BLESS YOU.

BRAVE ON THE ROCKS begins about 6 MONTHS after Spilling Open First came out... when the pressure on myself to ~~BE MORE~~ BE MORE - GIVE MORE SHARE MORE Love more was Building so big that the TOPPiling over

Was soon to come.

Dearest Sprout,

I drift through your evocative work as if in a dream. Your meld of image and color and word surprises my heart and brings back the many rich moments we have shared together: the magic of our "explores," holding your little head back to feel snow fall upon your face, the special wave we invented to greet passing trains at Westmount Station. Best of all, I recall the tactile sensation of our barefoot adventures at DeGrassi Point.

Up at our family cottage everybody goes around in bare feet. It's been that way for over a hundred years. Barefoot travel allows you to get the true feel of a place. Hot sun on the grass, worn roots, slabs of pre-Cambrian granite. When I was a kid the best "secret trail" was the narrow path along the lake once used by Indians who brought their quill- and beadwork to the cottages every August. In the old days it was called the Indian Path and it used to go all the way to the Creek, where I watched baby painted turtles sun themselves on lily pads.

Just before you were born the Creek was dredged and new cottages were constructed right on top of the Indian Path. By the time you were ready to discover "secret trails" of your own, the Creek had become a marina, and even a small stretch of the original path was so overgrown it was hard to find.

The summer you turned six you were undaunted. You were obsessed with secret trails and you pleaded with me to show you as many as I could remember. There were a couple of great ones out on Pine Ridge where I used to build tree forts with my cousins. I remember there was another one you especially loved behind the McMurrich boathouse.

The best trail of all was still the Indian Path, and sometimes at sunset we'd find it and walk along together, usually on the way back from swimming on the sandbars. We'd cross over the Frog Bridge and head up the road to your granddad's driveway, which he had covered that summer with two tons of new gravel.

The thing about bare feet is that they move easily and quickly over mud and dirt and sand and grass but tend to hesitate before a barrier of pointy, sharp-edged gravel.

As a little girl you used to hold your arms up for a "special carry," and this is what you did the first time we reached the gravel. But in this situation something told me not to pick you up. It's odd how I can see the moment so clearly, even today.

In my mind's eye I see myself hunker down in front of you and explain the rules of barefoot travel. I told you paths are not always smooth and familiar like the Indian Trail or the good ones out on Pine Ridge. Sometimes there are rocks on the trail and the only way to cross them is to be brave.

As I sit here so many years later, I smile when I remember how proudly you walked over the gravel that summer. Whenever we came back to the cottage by way of the Frog Bridge, you would get breathless and boldly announce how you were going to be "brave on the rocks."

Love,
Dad

"GOD calls you to the place WHERE your deep Gladness + tHE World's Deep Hunger MEEt." — FREDERICK BUECHNER

⭐ IT IS exciting and strange to Be
BRave For everyone who
WAnts to know- to connect

Who feels these same
ACHes.
I do want to help.

THIS Begins here
Sometimes I feel isolated
even more Because
readers may think that now
Because I am published...
The aches....
THE Questions...
and the doubts-
MUSt VANish...
not so Quickly.

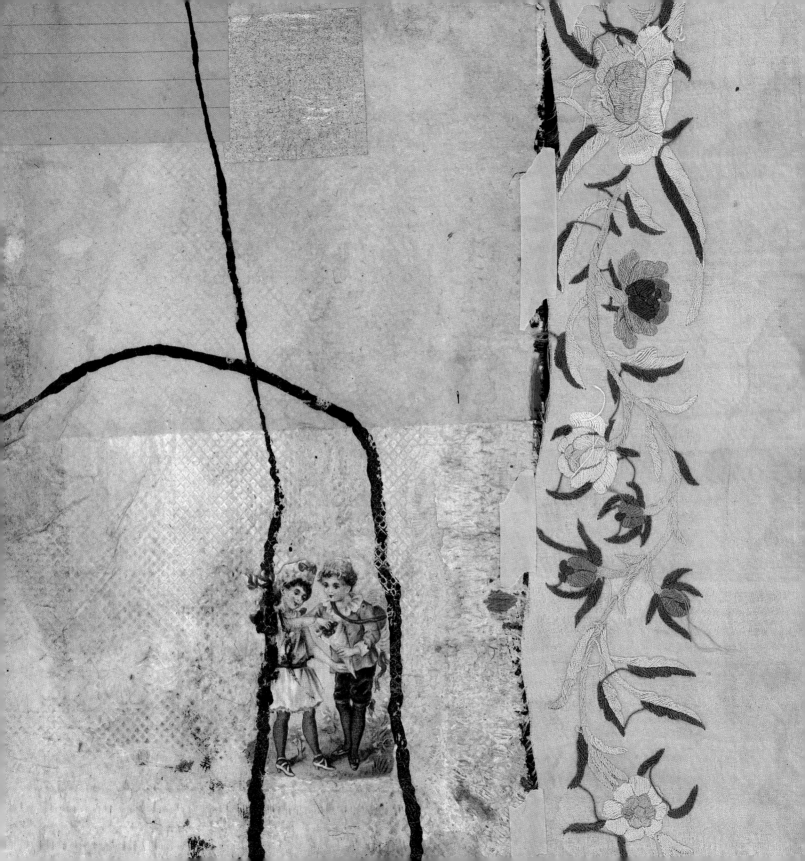

Yesterday I was
Disintegrating...
tHERE is so much
pressure I put
on myself to
feel different
thAN HOW I feel.
TO BE ~~MOA~~
MORE
Joyous,
complete,
Loose

Bed.

Photo By Amanda Marsalis

ROSES

STUCK
FILLED
up
in Here

for my mom.

* sometimes
i feel
the "thing"
i'm trying to
give to the
~~not~~ world.

sometimes
i just don't
GIVE
it to
myself.

I HAVE TO BE ever
so gentle with the Hope
I woke up with today...
maybe today? maybe. now?

I lit candles
and made tea.

Alysson said to me the other night,
"You HAVE had success at
expressing yourself...That is
the greatest success."

Now do I keep doing this? - For
myself -
For others?

do I have to?

WHAT can remain my own Questions?
expectations!!! AHH these Bitter Boys!
I thought By now I wouldn't
feel so unsure about my
choices.

1
2
3
4
5
6
7
8
9

Natural Waistline
Taille normale
Cintura normal
Cintura normal

Pleat
Pli

I still get flashes
OF "OH it's All WRONG!"
~~Your~~ voices in my ➤ head say:
"wrong Way to spend
my Time"
WRONG I'm not teaching now
WRONG Body
wrong relationship
WRONG HOUSE
wrong wrong wrong.
I don't KNOW
what these days
I can SAY I
"KNOW FOR SURE"

I do know that I'm
here in this chilly wind
Looking closely and
feeling the feelings
OF my AgE.

Lilli—True + dear
1992.
LILLI

Not Mine Not Mine nope Ain't Mine

HOW CAN I DO it all?

WE GIVE GIVE away

the only way out is through —R. FROST

sometimes
I Feel really
In The ~~SPOT~~
   Spot Light
   and i'm not ~~acting~~ acting.
RIGHt.
      Sometimes I feel like
I AM   mean to people who
   Love me.

      sometimes I just want to
   Be more sweet and
               funny.

      sometimes   I Break.

HOOKED
TOGETHER
Life.

I HAVE A HARD time
connecting and loving
all of MY selves and
THE different moments of
my LIFE so FAR
HOW CAN all these
parts OF ME Be one?

everyone wants
to put everyone
into a BOX
just the way
they
want
you

I feel
Lonely in
my body
right
now.

will you DANCE WITH ME

I haven't written in my journal alone here with myself FOR the real reasons in a long TIME.

Tonight it's → MY OWN BOOK for myself. No sharing it with the World tonight!

it is just here Rickety, lonesome and CALM.

I am carrying so much (tension) what is it for?

{the BETTERNESS COMPLEX}

One thing I've Been noticing building in Me is THE Betterness COMPLEX

(I like to call it that)

"All Ways" striving — never soaking.

everything I will never do again.

· pretend I'm "Okay" when I feel terrible

· Laugh when It's not Funny

· WHISPER WHEN — I need to speak up. SPEAK UP. Speak up

read RUMI's poem "THE Guest HOUSE"

and PEMA CHÖDRÖN's BOOK When Things Fall APART Shambhala Books

i've Been
waking up less
Alive these days.
It scares me.

I haven't Been Free
Sorta Numb to life
or really myself.

CONCERNED

PAIN
SOAKING
IN.

WORRIES I'VE HAD

tangled hair

losing everything...

FIRE

Abandonment

being Yelled at

Not being able to "Handle it all"

NO MORE FAITH

No ideas

disappointing someone I love

Not Being funny enough

NOT BEING BRAVE ENOUGH

being very Very lonely

LIVING up to too high expectations

sometimes I FEEL CLOSED up in A TRUNK of fear... tiny in the world

SOMETIMES I WASTE TOO MUCH TIME WORRYING about being HURT AND IT DOESN'T PROTECT Me.

sometimes I really leave the tiny afraid girl inside all alone Betraying myself again and again.

Last night
→ I dreamed of a BAT being
cAught in My room against
My light. I couldn't get it out I
WAS scared to cATch II

I feel SAD PIN·PRICK·ACHE.
SORE SIDE
Weak weak

falling star in my
ROOM.
my lights are
all off.

ULCER (ŭl'sər) N.   ULcer

1 ulcer, a lesion of the skin or a mucous membrane
such as the one lining the stomach that is
accompanied by formation of pus and necrosis
F surrounding tissue, usually resulting from
NFLAMMation or ischemia
2ULcer A corrupting condition or influence.

Angry.
tireD
aggressive
Mad

confused. in love. in HATE.
PUSHing AWAY. wanting
CLOSE. Pissed. overcome.
HURTing. wanting
escape. and freedom.
DREAM: turbulent ocean, shark FINS
THROUGh my FLOOR, cutting me up,
my privacy, my comfort.
What do i have to see?
WHERE do i have to go?
Learn that.

i am

falling

The PAIN came BACK
In my Tummy, WHAT
is It Really? Ulcers—
Ulcers Ulcers

alex's words of "SABRINA I told my MOM
YOU HAVE an Ulcer" and without missing
A BEAT SHE SAID "SHE HAS GOT
TO PUT it all someWHERE.
→ so what am I holding in so Tightly?

HAS too MUCH passed to even begin
to share what hurts so much?
THE DOUBtS HURt.

worry worry worry worry worry worry worry.
I put it in my journals—
I didn't speak up.

worry worry!

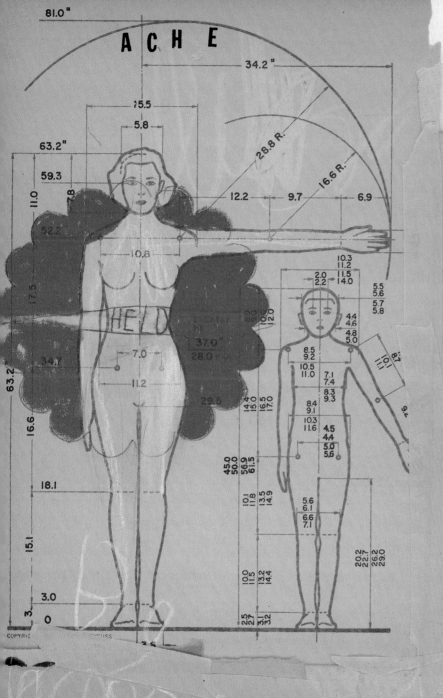

ACHE

where am I putting
it all away?
why?

Sometimes I feel there
isn't room to FALL.
why can I give to
Others — calm, peace,
encouragement — yet
not to ~~myself~~ Myself?

I leave ~~myself~~
Myself here alone

and achy, Filled up

with my own harsh
voices.

Be more. Be more. Be more.

I want Health and HEALING, and holding close. I want TREASURES. I want similar souls. I want passionate YESes I want to BE BLOWN AWAY. I want to trust. I want calm glad-ness. and prayers and Deep TRUE BREATH. talks

Megan has gone
home
· Tymaree WENT camping
SAra moved
Alex is in BRAZiL
and I'm
in the Backyard
reading
Anne Lamott.
and filing my
NEGATIVes....

gotta go explore.

SAB + Alex. OAKland '99

I wonder "people travel to at the height of mountains, at the huge waves of the sea, at the long course of rivers, and they pass by themselves — without wondering"

--St. Augustine

trust yourself. leave ripples.

I want to get
Lost.
I want to find meaning
alone by myself

→ AN
exploration
that will take
me FAR and
WidE.

BARE. ~~empty~~

I must go!
   where shall
I begin?

Lost is where
I'll BE FOUND.
ITALY

I want to hear Jazz with my eyes closed, and dig my toes into the sand dancing. I want to climb to the Summit and Yell, and sleep under the stars. I want to Laugh my head off and play marbles and sleep in and eat croissants in bed, with Butter and Marmalade and spill coffee and wear Lace and trip holding your hand because I am Listening so closely.

☆go to erykah BADU.
   Ani DiFranco
      concerts.
   DRIVE across U.S.A.
   go through CANADA
   BACK to COTTAGE.
   visit Anna in
   Washington.

<u>CALL GET TICKET</u>
LIVE/WORK community
      (visit cell space in S.F.)

Mills residency?
Laney College?
   Call Back Jason +
            Trathen.
   pick up negatives.
at <u>Looking Glass</u>
I want to get myself
   to Italy SOON!

SHE HAD HOPING EYES THAT LOOKED FARTHER THAN SHE KNEW.

→ this is A trip I must make alone, to Italy. I am at my breaking POINT these days

feeling THIS OFTEN → "Uhhh! this is so chaotic' I Need help" please.

GOD please provide me with that HELP to get me GONE — really GONE AWAY

[TRATHONS Soup Plan]
~~Beet~~ FOR ULCERS.
BEETS
potato peel
carrots
garlic
DARK greens
celery.
potASSium
BROTH ☆

I want the ulcers to GO AWAY.

I am going to ITALY FOR my own summer. summer is just beginning form I am going to awaken to my voice again. Recolor with yellow light and perfect, PERFECT Sea. I am going to Italy to wander. I AM going to ITALY Because it is there and I am Here.

I am going to Italy FOR myself. I want to give this to you Sabrina to heal my hurting INSIDES Undo the knot and Reach up to the sky. my arms I am going to ITALY.

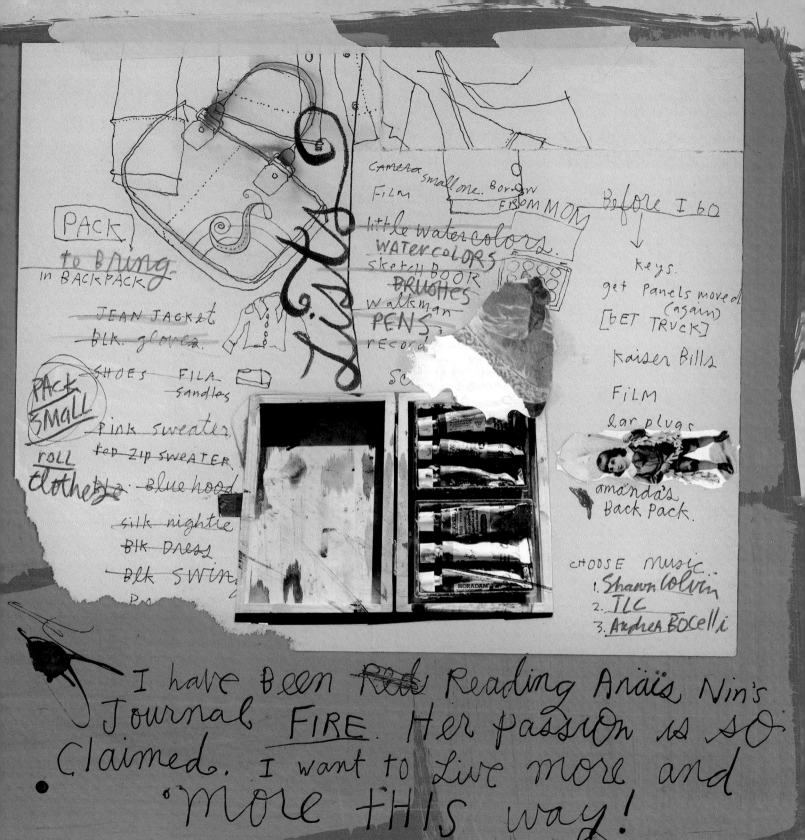

PACK
to bring.
IN BACKPACK

JEAN JACKET
blk. gloves.

PACK
SMALL

roll
clothes

SHOES FILA
Sandles

Pink sweater
red zip SWEATER
blue hood.

silk nightie
BlK DRESS
Blk SWIM

Camera small one. Borrow
FILM   FROM MOM
little watercolors.
WATERCOLORS
sketch book
BRUSHES
Walkman
PENS,
record

Before I go
↓
keys.
get panels moved.
(again)
[GET TRUCK]

kaiser bills

FILM
ear plugs

amanda's
Back Pack.

CHOOSE music.
1. Shawn Colvin
2. TLC
3. Andrea Bocelli

I have been Reading Anäis Nin's
Journal FIRE. Her passion is so
Claimed. I want to live more and
MORE tHIS way!

Photo Amanda Marsalis

GOD help ME. I am scared. I feel caught
IN MY THROAT—tight and exhausted.
    I leave tomorrow!!
(I feel like a cannonBALL before it
is shot into the wide sky.) Susan told
ME today that I AM supposed to feel this way
before an adventure. this is PART OF IT.
SEPARATION part of the choice I had to make.
(IT IS HARD to let GO and let GOD.)

Do ut Be afrad
you can dort

note from — Mari

WITH NOTHING to learn, NOTHING
TO FIGURE-Out, NO MYSTERIES, THOUGHTS,-
-IF THERE IS No knowledge, No Fear,

OR No love, —

THERE IS (NO) lIFE.

by Hannah

italy

Let go

I feel so shy
and scared and the
plane hasn't even left
yet.

HERE we go sabrina

(I am proud of myself
and have an excitement
in my soul Quivering)
Yes sabrina yes yes
yes.
I feel Life
rushing
FORWARD

Leaving going... pulling away

gone

a mixture
of sadness
attachment
and release

I am going ... to Italy

to listen to my own voice

I am going to Italy

to italy because it is there

TO ITALY FOR MYSELF. I want

To heal my hustling

knots and reach my

I am going to italy

for my/our summer
happen are color with
perfect purple sky
to wander here I am going
and I am here I am going
to give thy to you Sabrina
inside undo the
arms into the sky
8.31.99.

Berkeley, California.

arriving

FREE

Find.

Just Looking

Home inside

ROME

20 zillion HOURS Later

CHAOTIC BACKPACK carrying through the Airport Trainstations and vespa vespa Filled streets of ROME

I'm really Here now.

AMAZING THAT

trying to find Gullivers' HOUSE HOSTEL

BED NEeDeD.

2

1

* met
Bill + Susi
on plane over Here.
they are on their
Honeymoon...
funny good Folks.

2.   3.   4.

WALking + WALKing and walking

(I WANt to Drop THIS BACKPACK NOW

5.

4

OH...THE Colors of THIS city

Letters to my son By Kent Nerburn

traveling.

To be a real traveler you must be willing to give yourself over to the moment and take yourself out of the center of your universe. You must believe totally in the lives of the people and the places where you find yourself, even if it causes you to lose faith in the life you left behind.

You need to share with them, participate with them. Sit at their tables, go to their streets. Struggle with their language. Tell them stories of your life and hear the stories of theirs. Watch how they love each other, how they fight each other. See what they value and what they fear. Feel the spaces they keep in their lives.

Become part of the fabric of their everyday lives and you will get a sense of what it means to live in their world. Give yourself over to them — embrace them rather than judge them — and you will find that the beauty in their lives and their world will become part of yours.

When you move on, you will have grown. You will

It began in ROME. a tiny church. Quiet
And I am overcome with tears and heat.
such exhaustion in a dizzy daze.
crying For the Beauty. THE scale OF this
City. angels surround me BARE feet 3 nuns
I AM in ITALY I AM in italy. Next DAY NOW Full night of sleep

I AM A bullivers HOUSE
waiting to Leave for EUROSTA
the TRAIN RIDE to tuscany.

painting JUST FOR MYSELF

CASTLES

we'm really on
the
train to FLORENCE
in A GLORIOUS HOT DAY
passing little downs
it's funny
i don't
feel far
From home. my loves are
so close in
my heart.

You are home.

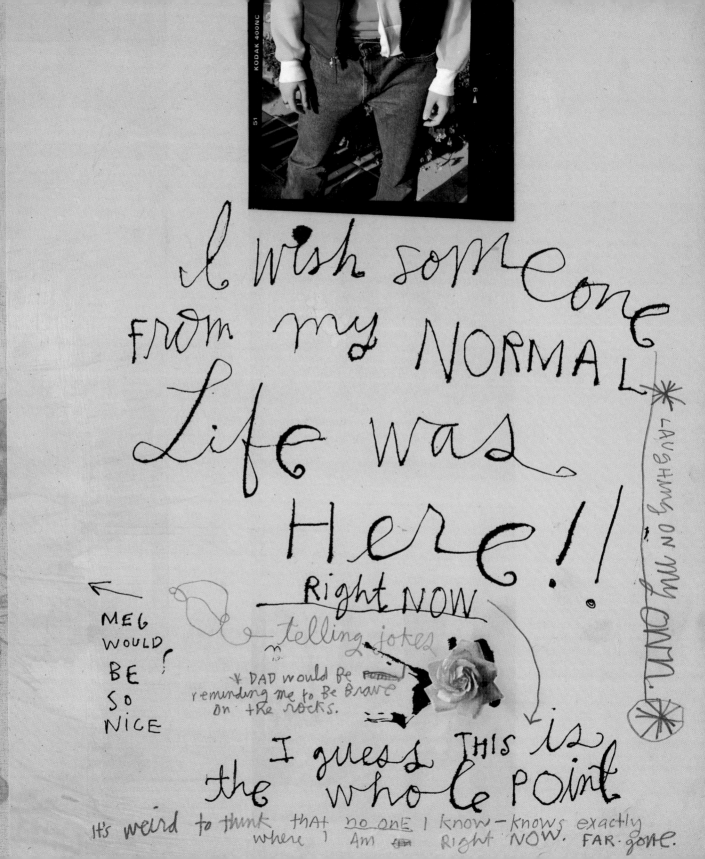

I wish someone
from my NORMAL
Life was
Here!!

Right NOW
telling jokes

MEG
WOULD
BE
SO
NICE

* DAD would be
reminding me to Be Brave
on the rocks.

LAUGHING ON MY OWN.

I guess This is
the whole POINT

It's weird to think that no one I know - knows exactly
where I AM   RIGHT NOW. FAR-gone.

WHAT I REMEMBER

SEPTEMBER

september 24th, 1999. sitting Quietly so... calm in my body just Quiet time alone

I cant believe I've only been here 3 days! really what I have absorbed into my heart so is such... peace and contentment with life fair it is my enchanted April. here to SOAK

TUSCANY

yesterday, at my breaking point of exhaustion and lunliness she said "up, up... put your shoes on, were going to get icecream!" we were out the door and wandering the little streets, Romans bustling around getting fresh pasta and veggies for dinner

I
AM
EXHAUSTED.

I need FOOD
I NEED REFUELING
WHAT IS gonna
happen THIS week?

choose your OWN
ADVENTURE

sept 25th

- GRAPE Vine Roots
- deep hard soil churned up in A Vineyard.
  ~~Fee~~ (Feels Like my Life NOW)

HOT
humid
OVERCAST.

- TONi
- Kerryn
- Bonnie

good gals
Ive met
so far

Quiet Walks finally.
I Need this solitude.
Just hearing the sound of
the pencil move across
THE PAPER.
~~Fir~~ First real moment feeling on my own.
I sit here on this Red PARK Bench.
alley cats in the sun... Fermented grapes
on the Road — it is wine season
RIPE grapes. BASKets On shoulders.
perfect.

I want to give myself permission to take my time on this Adventure.

my tummy ~~hurts~~ hurts Today.

ITALY ✻

Florence I am awake very early
on my first morning in Florence
(took the train here yesterday)
— up early to get a bed at the Hostel
(Archi Rossi)
And I DID it, I was packed up and checked into
the new spot by 7:30 am.

I feel more settled
than yesterday.
Last night I walked
in a daze through the city until
I Fell Asleep.
I am trying to notice the small things, like
the sunrise pink over the city of red.
Tiled roofs, where a cat sat in the rooftop
. Sun. I watched from the little window
in My shower.

tiny.

I don't have to "Rush to keep moving" to avoid the Loneliness.
I went to check my e-mail and THE NETWORK wasn't connecting. (GOD WORKS IN funny WAYS)
I shouldn't BE IN AN INTERNET CAFE trying to "connect".

• GOTTA WASH THESE CLOTHES
• get FACE SOAP

I should Be in the streets of THIS ~~my~~ Magnificent City

• OHH funny hair of mine – can't pull OFF the sleek ITALIAN Look!

BOBBi-PINS HELP A Bit.

I HAVE met great women. TRAVELING alone for similar reasons –

• escape
• strength

DISCOVERING the great uses OF SCARVES on your head. Helps — Funny HAIR DAYS after Days.

• to find something Lost.

TOMORROW i will leave for Florence and begin my explores in that magnificent city. I am ready for museums and conversations.

I have to close my eyes and feel myself here inside this experience.

IN THE RAIN we scurry along. Little grapples from chickens on bikes. I am sitting in a little candy and great store. generations of women are working and storytelling here. There are wild down—

quiet times in gentle riding

SO LONG LEONARD COHEN

CITY WALK

SABOS

I'm SO NOT Italian!

what I've noticed about them:
  1. Italians are SHOCKingly Beautiful.
      Quite tall
      Quite Beautifully BRONZED (not too many freckles
      and Very Stylish.   around here.)
  The wrinkled Balledup Black skirt just isn't pulling it off.
  it's Better THAN SHORTs and a FANNY PACK FOR me ← THOUGH.
      NO EXTRA Butt BULK!

spill
#42 →

The colors people wear: rich greens, reds,
golden TONes. I have Bought a wild
Italian LONG skirt that inspires me
TO MAKE the skirts I've Been dreaming of
SINCE I was Little.
    ... why did we all stArt wearing
        BlAck in the '90's? RECOLOR
      put the color BACK ON.

Long skirts Are all I really want to wear here

when I get HOME
I WANT TO MAKE
SOME.

The Long
Skirt Dream
the
WANDERing wear

Size 12 38½

B

D

ENUE, NEW YORK, NEW
PRINTED

Bor
May

BRAVE
ON THE
ROCKS

soon we wil
together

I LOVE roaming
THROUGH this
Country in
Long skirts
simple
tank tops
and sandals SANDALS
and, of course
the
scarf
on
my
head.
A spot
of color

TAKE OFF
THE TOO
tight
clothes
and too
High Boots.
no jeans
Are Happening
FOR me
HERE.
Lovely and
Loose.

SABRINA
Skirts

looking
faster

maybe handwriting
on the skirt!

lots of differ

Little TOPS in TUSCANY.

where have you been?

where are you needing?

simple dress

I feel more feminine here than I have before.
This culture is rich with energy, and
strength. WOMEN ARE APPRECIATED, Respected, full COLOR.
AS A WOMAN HERE I FEEL STRONG. There
IS AN immediate connection to other women I meet,
A feeling OF "OH YES...YOU TOO are taking this Adventure FOR
Yourself."

F a r t h e r

IN MY Life ONE DAY...

- A trAin to tuscany.
- belly dancE
- drive across U.S.A.
- PARIS in the Spring.
- SALSA DANCE
- Live with A tuB
- Live with A Balcony.
- have A BABy.
- Live In A Live/Work SPAcE

I Found THis old NAPkin in MY Journal WRitten MontHs before THis TRiP.

I wrote it at Cafe dü Nord in SanFrancisco — Out DANcing. It Feels really good TO Be living into THESE DREAMS

＊ KEEP Going.

I feel
SO
STRONG.
WHEN I
feel this WAY
I can
HANDLe
Anything.
I AM
not AFRAID
Of Life
Hurting
ME.

THE WALK THROUGH THE CITY AT NIGHT. MOON hitting the ☆ Cafe Mokamag ❂ 10:2 roof tops and sculptures it was a city underwater, evening. 2 it was a city underwater REFLECTED IN WANDERING the RIVER. through floren LAMP POSTS and lights ON THE RIVER. BEFORE SUNRIS deep blu night

SALVATORE

ARIS...ULA

TEVERE FARNESIN

LUNGOTEVERE TEBALDI

CONVALIDA

Mod. 713/TL-9
Cod. T.39/9/1A.2(60)

Via Regionale
...RIA

my mind eye

LAUGH
till
my cheeks hurt and
THEN SOME MORE
"the French girl"
late sun
TUSCANY
last VIEWS full up

all the people sharing all the world

~~Amalfi~~ AMALFI COAST

*collecting THE colorful tiles On the BeAch that TRATHEN told me about before I left. go and see

TRUST WHAT IS Beyond our sight.

I HAVE BEEN touched BY Lives I didn't know existeD.

epiphanies

THE Bus drivers giving directions, waiters feeding me WELL, travelers sharing A TRAIN ride. people Living their Lives Beside mine is only for a minute, I am TOUCHED BY the extra CARE they give.

~thank you~

SHAWN Colvin's A FEW SMALL REPAIRS ALBUM is Perfect on the TRAIN.

coniliner

Zipping along the Riviera on a motorcycle in a Bikini singing U2 Songs out loud. My friend Pepe has Been a good source for HISTORY And stories of this AREA. HE GREW up his whole 🐟 Life here in Amalfi.

I told HIM I WAS engaged so there would Be NO ProBlem.→ (they don't take "I have A Boyfriend" AS A WARNING.)

→ ITAlian men are frisky Ones!

✳ They WORK that Romantic thing to the TOP! At Times Like this I miss and forget what Being a GIRLFRIEND is Like. It feels DISTANT from here. Even though I have met many BOYS here, my heart is not involved TO the SAME degree— in the PARTNERShip degree. IT feels good to have this independence in My BODy. Fully SABRINA STRONG.

TAKE THIS HOME with me.!!

sea

~The VIEW.

THE VIEW

the widest sea I've ever seen.
THROUGH CROOKED STAIRWAYS
going this way and tHAT ———
to a church AND stairs that
lead out, out and away

{remember this Sabrina.}

THE sun rose here, after saying goodnight
BACK HOME.
                    I like being Quiet
                AND NOT hearing
            ENGLish BEING SPOKEN.
Healing BODY.
softening in.
Quiet
——————→ just Looking ←————

I feel like the only guest in this
    little town of Atrani. it's not —→ FLASHY.
It's BEAUTY is simple + stunning in
[its]→BARE AND peeling WALls against
    the sea.

OPENING

cats wander, people carry on.

sea

textures of time gone By.

ATRANI ITALY.

✳ The mornings HERE Bring so much curiosity. everyone is going about their business, starting their day. IT is different than the U.S.A., more Beautifully BASIC.

Bring in the fishing BOATs with Fish For the DAY. "BUONO GIORNOS" everywhere. GOOD MORNING. The days Begin before sunrise. I Like to watch the fishermen in their BOATs alone on the SEA. They must have such conversations with themselves. Watching the old Ladies PASS the church Blowing kisses. I like so very much to Be ALone to take this in.

But I sometimes yearn for companionship with another. I see women here on "ITALian TOURS" with SCOWLS on their FACES,

gripping onto their MAN's hand,
Him always leading the way
RUSHING FROM FAMOUS FOUNTAIN to CLASSIC SCULPTURE... TAKING pictures- pictures!!
So much SNAPPING pictures
FOR PROOF — what kind
of proof?
I don't believe in Traveling
tHis way. ———> But this is
their proof. and I guess we
all need our different proof tHAt
WE HAVE done "our own Adventure"
things i've just   never tried
              (MINE NEEDED tO BE
              The BIKINI and VesPA
              racing down the COAst proof.)

.I feel so far from being   SABRINA WARD HARRISON
sometimes the   for anyone   TODAY.
bravest tHings Are the most simple in
                                              the end
         I AM Lost. I AM FOUND.

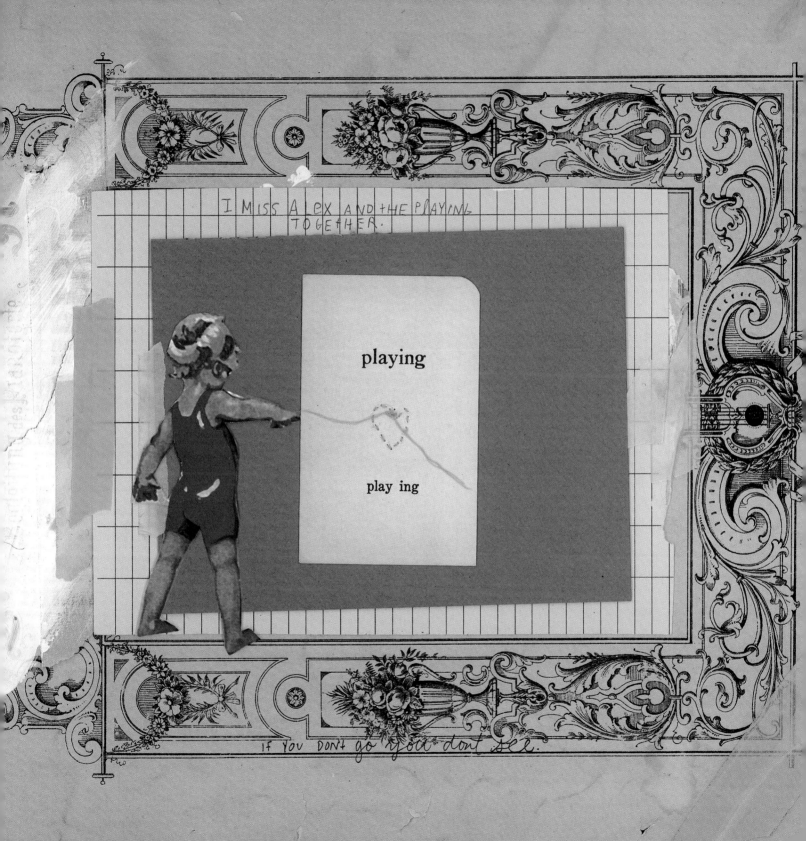

I MISS ALEX AND THE PLAYING TOGETHER.

playing

play ing

If you don't go you don't see.

Atrani

FISHER MEN.
AT SEA.

I feel so different than when I left. The aching girl who felt so burnt out and Lost in her OWN SELF HAS HEALED. Something has shifted in me. I like to sit here Quietly just Holding my journal and gazing Out to sea. I feel myself filling BACK up again, able to give LOVE in my Life again. To relationships, to myself, and perhaps A BOOK. ⟶ IT WOULD START out so honest about the SIX MONTHS after Spilling Open emerged

THe BOOK would speak of my ulcers AND WHAT it took to (heal) myself. Sometimes the sickness itself is the wakeup call to have the adventure. TO see myself FAR and wide Alone and Becoming Strong

Love found

(HOW RANDOM tHAt I MAKE these Books)

SAB. 2. book

That is why we need to travel. If we don't offer our-
selves to the unknown, our senses dull. Our world
becomes small and we lose our sense of wonder. Our
eyes don't lift to the horizon; our ears don't hear the
sounds around us. The edge is off our experience, and we
pass our days in a routine that is both comfortable and
limiting. We wake up one day and find that we have lost
our dreams in order to protect our days.

Don't let yourself become one of these people. The
fear of the unknown and the lure of the comfortable will
conspire to keep you from taking the chances the traveler
has to take. But if you take them, you will never regret your
choice. To be sure, there will be moments of doubt when

Kent Nerburn

under
Italian
skies?

MASSEMO
FONTANA
23

I HAVE needed this solitude to go badly. I
this solo adventure. is what my
craving. And when I am hee
is when I really
need to

Its just nic my music and the wide
horizon AHEAD. September 27, 99

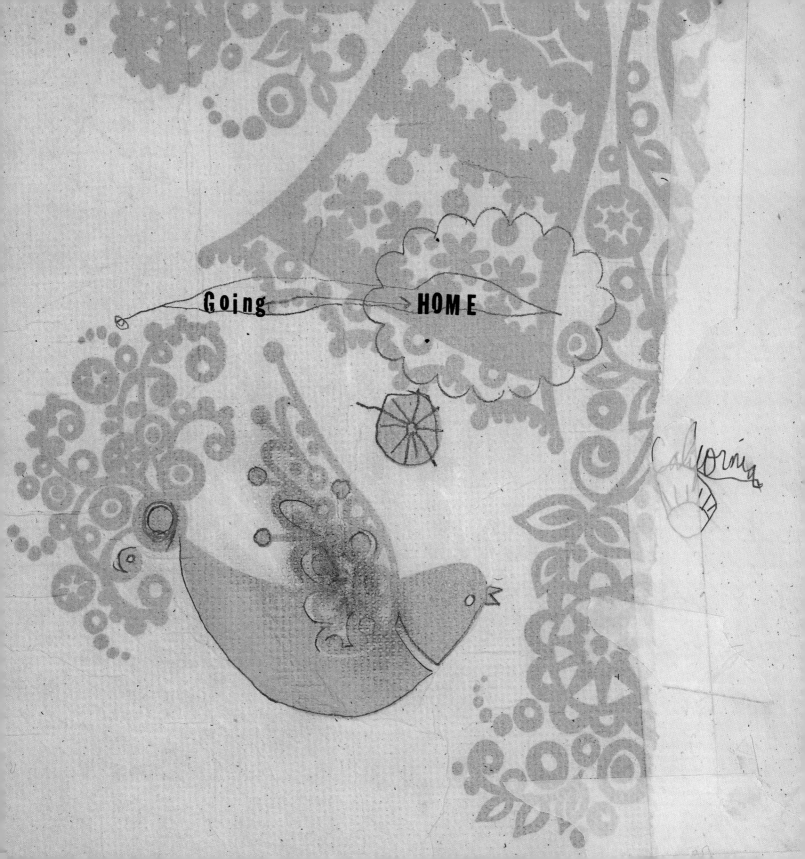

* flying Back
40 minutes to go
~~till~~ till home

I feel a surge in me to
remember all I have
learned on this journey
I know it Will leak out over
the NEXT days and MONTHS.
I HAVE LEARNED to WAIT A Little
Longer, That I CAN TAKE
MY Life ON MY BACK
in my BACKPACK.
I LEARNED that I can
sit by the sea and MAKE HOME!. I
learned I could make due with
I used to think I was Not capable
I reconnected to MY peers, to
WOMEN FROM All over THE WORLD

trust yourself.

FOR MYSELF

WE ARE all
so similar.

situations
of.

Listening to messages on a payphone at ~~this~~ the airport, my smile spread so wide. I saw my grin in the reflection of the payphone.

calls
· susan
· alex
· Megan
Tymaree home.
· Jason

FAMILIAR VOICES.

It feels exciting to BE BACK. Life feels FRESH.

ME TODAY
* SuperMAN T-shirt
* Pink scarf on head
delight + giddy
excited to see
MOM + DAD
I feel so young
and so old.
BRAVE

I close my eyes and still feel ITALY in MY BODY and on MY HANDS.

♡ THANK YOU GOD FOR THIS GIFT. the most beautiful time of MY life ON MY OWN.

I DID it I DID it.

It was a funny moment sitting ON THE TWA PLANE ready to TAKE off for HOME. THE MOVIE screen came DOWN AND THEY ——→ were showing safety info and the normal PLANE STUFF. THEN a song STARTED PLAYING "There SHE GOES" and a MUSIC video WAS ON THE MONITORS. (since WHEN did they start playing MUSIC Videos ON AIRPLANES?) I LOOKED UP AND WITH SHOCK I SAW MYSELF, MY PAINTINGS ——→ IT WAS THE SIX PENCE NONE the RICHER VIDEO I HAD RANDOMLY gottEN THE JOB to DO the ART FOR and sorta PLAY the ARTIST in the VIDEO. And here IT WAS— playing on this PLANE???? MY NECK TURNED RED WITH BLUSHING. These weeks of feeling Lost and found AND THEN WHAM BACK. Doing that video PROJECt WAS the Last + Biggest thing I did before my ulcer fully HIT. I HAD Pushed myself too FAR and too FAST. I WASN'T even able to enjoy the moment or see the FiLMing of the video. I HAD gotten so sick. It WAS AFTER this that I KNEW I couldn't MAKE ARt THIS WAY ANYMORE. THE PRESSURE I WAS PUTTING ON MYSELF WAS insane —AND IT JUST

WASN'T WORTH IT ANYMORE

HOW CAN IT BE DIFFERENT NOW?

HOW can I take care of myself —

NOT ~~XXXX~~ LOSE myself all over again.

{ OVERWELMED so often. }

(are you too?)

HAS ITALY MADE IT go away? forever?

CAN I HOLD THINGS

A Little Looser NOW?

Lighten MY LOAD OF expectations. to

~~BE MORE~~
~~give more~~
~~MAKE MORE~~
share MorE
Tell MorE
gLow MorE

EXPECTATIONS

Just too Many
and way too soon

FOR NOW on the plane —

it WAS A simple Blushing reminder of the

excitement AS Well AS the

CHALLENGE.

THE THAN... ...LLS FROM
THE STAR... ...BURY...
WAIT. SO... BILL RO...
FLIGHT AND FIRST
TRAIN. SIMON AND
ICECREAM FOR
TEARS. ALISON
FROM T.O. CO...
RELATE TO ACHE...
TONI FROM LA
AMBITION TO ESCAPE TRAVELING DEAR.
TUSCANY VILLA DAPHNE QUEEN
OLD ITALIAN LADY ON MY MORNING
WALK. CASTLE. RESTURAUNT FIRST
SALMONE PENNE AND SEE KASIS.
BONNIE FROM SIDNEY. SAME +
ALIVE. OAKLAND PAIR. CINQUE TERRE
RIDE CENTRAL BAR ROOM
TERRACE WARM RAIN EXPLORES
MASSIMO + TONI YOGA BY MOON
LIGHT. DIVINE PESTO PIZZA. RIDE
SANTA MARGERITA PASTRI LADIES.
PIANO BAR. PIZZA MAKER. ROOM
OF MY OWN. BATH. BATH. CUTTY
SARK DINNER. SKIRT SHOP.
AUSTRALIAN LADIES GREEN SPATS
GOING to FLORENCE.

Stella Ma...

ALIKE- ROOM. e-MAILS FROM
BOBBI AND M + D. TINY PIAZZA
FAL. THE SUN CAFÉ CHAIR
WIND. SALVATORE RESCUE
LUNCH. LEMONAN PAINTINGS.
TOUR. LIME COOKING. VESPA
AND HERDOES. BRITISH LADY
TOURIST SHIRT. BEADS. BUGS
JOHNNY BALDIN. CHINESE.
VALLOMBROSA. FRENCH & IRL. BUS
RIGHT IN FLORENCE BEFORE
SUNRISE. T.C. SHAWN COLVIN.
PIZZA. AMALFI ATRANI. FILLIP D.
PIZZA. CATS IN THE SUN. PEPPE
BABINI RIDES. SEA HIGH
LADIES. N KATIE. J N N Y. E D

"But I give Life. I can rarely wield Death. Yet I have the power to destroy. Life. FIRE. NEVER DEATH. Fire + Life. Le jue." Anais Nin

{ Megan B.
me.
Megan R.
Molly F.

HOME*

Nina Pratt's photo

BACK at the ITALian Resturant,
around THE CORNER. HOME sweet home.
gifts of welcoming. wine + crab
I'M wearing my PINK scarf On my
HEAD and orange sneakers. I feel so good
I SAT in this seat by the WINDOW
with MARC Albert SO LOng ago....
Feeling Like a girl with a Big crush
AND OVERalls On → wanting to BE
A WISE solid WOman. with the
perfect
I AM A woman NOW — things
a SABrina growing OPEN to SAY.
and into HERSelf Bit·By·Bit.

PLANS
Of GOOD
THINGS
TO DO
BACKHOME

→ start yoga at ymca.
DANCING → (go see Lavay Smith
FALL WALKS call Nicki! in S.F.)
group → connect with LAurie WAGNER
KICK BOX
get access to a steam room
tea again. • BACK in my OWN warm Bed.

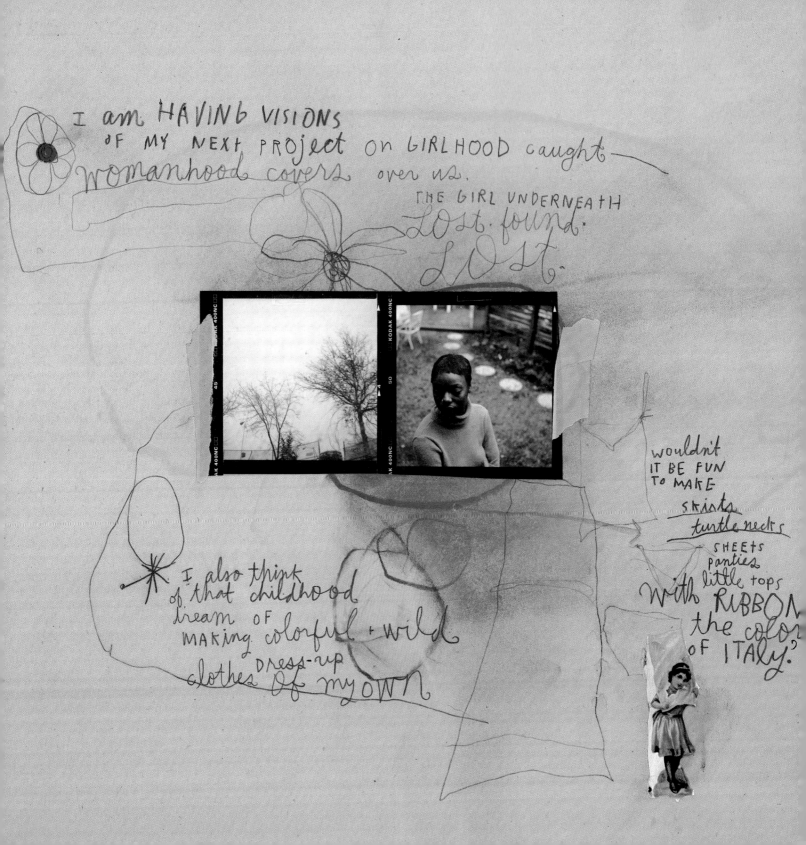

I am HAVING VISIONS
OF MY NEXT PROJECT ON GIRLHOOD caught —
womanhood covers over us.

THE GIRL UNDERNEATH
Lost. found.
LOST.

wouldn't
IT BE FUN
TO MAKE
skirts
turtlenecks
SHEETS
panties
little tops
with RIBBON
the color
OF ITALY.

I also think
of that childhood
dream of
MAKING colorful + wild
dress-up
clothes OF my OWN

I would never again be the same.

This is the magic of travel. Any travel. You leave your home secure in your own knowledge and identity. But as you travel, the world in all its richness intervenes. You meet people you could not invent; you see scenes you could not imagine. Your own world, which was so large as to consume your whole life, becomes smaller and smaller until it is only one tiny dot in time and space.

You return a different person.

All you need to do is give yourself over to the unknown. It doesn't have to be on a vast, dreamlike arctic plain. It can be on a gentle stroll through a Wisconsin forest or on a street corner in Nairobi. What matters is that you have left the comfort of the familiar and opened yourself to a world that is totally apart from your own.

Slowly the memories of the familiar recede from your mind and you find yourself adrift in the experience of the world around you. Your thoughts and concerns change. Your emotions focus on new people and events. The world makes its claim on your heart and mind, and you are free, at least momentarily, from the concerns of your everyday life.

Many people don't want to be travelers. They would rather be tourists, flitting over the surface of other people's lives while never really leaving their own. They try

KENt NERBURN

fabtastic

& museematic

I think of Italy and that
Quiet WATCHING I DID.
just TAKING in my experince
Filling up

I MISS THIS. I DO.

Life racing AHEAD

the VIEW is spectacular
tonight — perhaps falling   — STARS.

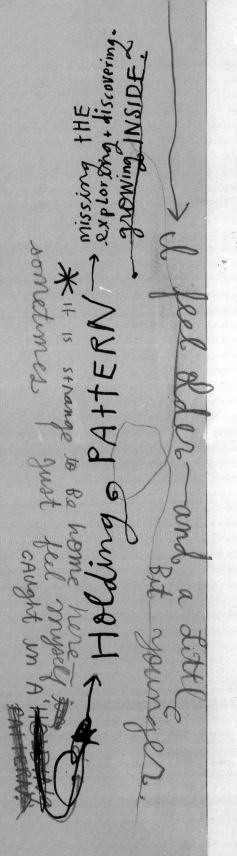

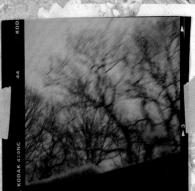

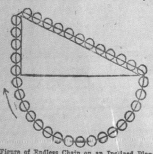

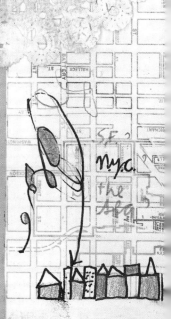

missing THE
exploring + discovering.
growing INSIDE.

it is strange to Be home here
sometimes I just feel myself caught in a 'holding' PATTERN.

I feel older—and a little bit younger.

Holding PATTERN

I Feel myself
Falling off again
REMEMBER
that
euphoria I
FELT THERE!
(keep it inside)

S.F.
n.y.c.
the sea

PERPETUAL 1072

Stevin proved the laws of the inclined plane by considering the arrangement shown in the figure of an endless chain hung over an inclined plane. Part of the chain hangs vertically, another and longer piece lies on the inclined plane, and the rest forms a sym-

Figure of Endless Chain on an Inclined Plane

metrical loop. The perpetual motionist argues that the part on the plane, being heavier, must pull up the vertical part, and that the whole must therefore move continuously in the direction of the arrow. The problem of perpetual motion is now clearly defined by science. To maintain any real machine in motion requires the expenditure of energy; the most perfect machine we can build will have some frictional resistance, and energy must be supplied to keep it in motion, and will be transformed into low-heat energy. A peculiar position is occupied by heat energy. This consists in the energy of motion of the atoms and molecules of bodies, and it can be converted into other forms of energy. The laws of this

AIR WATER

UPTHRUST OF WATER
MAKES IMMERSED
HALF OF WHEEL
APPARENTLY
LIGHTER

Diagram indicating idea of perpetual motion of a wheel, one half of which loses a certain amount of weight when immersed in water and no longer balances the other half which therefore pulls it round

conversion tell us that we can never make machines driven by heat energy unless we have a means for getting rid of part of the heat derived from our source of heat by dis-

motion, ... devise a ... able to ... moving from the faster-... air.

Per... city of se... p. 68, ... by a Sp... the ki... ... by the T... founde... 1324 ... com... the ... ... ress. There ... silk, woo...

Perra... ...70 wrote t... ... (stories ...

Persep... of t... pire, lying in a valley ... and its tributar... ruins. A new ... up... ruins, and began ... of Istakhr, in the ... and 7th cent. A.D. Portions ... have been excavated, in ... ception hall with forty co...

Perry, Bliss, 1860-1954, Am. author, was prof. of Eng. at Willia... 1886-93, prof. of oratory and aesthetic criticism at Princeton Univ. 1893-1900, editor of the Atlantic Monthly 1899. He was prof. of Eng. literature at Harvard Univ. 1907-30. His works include: A Study of Prose Fiction, 1902; The American Mind, A Study of Poetry, The Praise of Folly, Emerson Today, And Gladly Teach, 1935; also studies of Walt Whitman, Whittier, Carlyle, and three novels.

Perry, Oliver Hazard, 1785-1819, U.S. naval officer; served in the war with Tripoli; in 1809 commanded a fleet of gunboats at Newport, R. I. In the war of 1812 in the famous battle of Lake Erie, 1813, he captured the Br. fleet commanded by Capt. Barclay, and sent to Gen. Harrison his noted message 'We have met the enemy and they are ours.' By this victory Perry became a great natl. hero, and U.S. gained the control of Lake Erie. He was sent to the Mediterranean 1816-17, and to the W. Indies 1819 to protect Am. commerce. He contracted yellow fever and d. in Trinidad. There are monuments to his memory in Newport, R.I. and Put In Bay, Lake Erie.

Persephone, or Proserpine, in Gr. mythology, goddess of the underworld. Daughter of Zeus and Demeter, she was carried off by Pluto to the lower regions. Demeter secured her return for a part of each yr. by forbidding the earth to yield increase during her absence. She symboli...

ZONING MAP OF THE (

CARE tribe

NOB HILL SPECIAL USE DISTRICT

WASHINGTON - BROADWAY SPECIAL USE DISTRICT NO. 2

WASHINGTON - BROADWAY SPECIAL USE DISTRICT NO. 1

GARMENT SHOP SPECIAL USE DISTRICT

A B C D

SPECIAL USE DIST

change

where do i truly BELong.

Susan K.
Megan B.
Meg. R. Alex
Mim NANA + DAD Grandpa
Anna BECKY
Brian MIA
Nicki
Rebecca
Laura and my (BACK UP FAMily)
Hannah Lili
Megaan D. Nicki
TYMAREE Lamer + Anna
Jaysic + the castros
HElena PATRICK
Laurie
Chris J.
Opal
MArc
Jason
Trathen
Jennifer

OLD FAVORITES

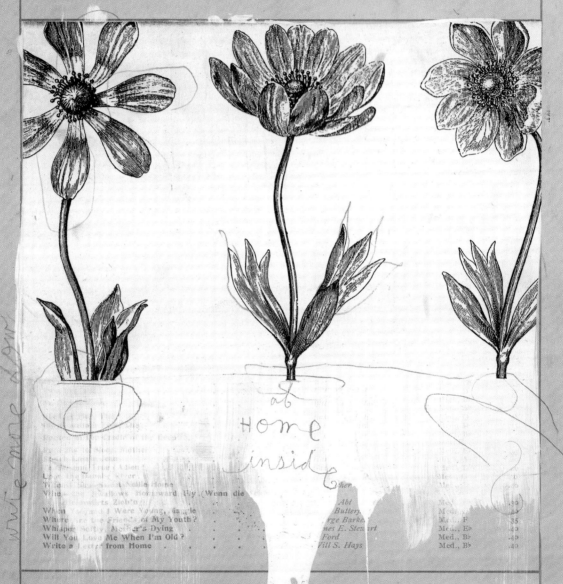

at
Home
inside

OLIVER DITSON COMPANY

NEW YORK
CHAS. H. DITSON & CO.

CHICAGO
LYON & HEALY

WHAT A YEAR 23 was!

~~what a year~~ → on the eve of 24!

Remembering

the first day of 23 —
coming HOME from Mexico — TO a
A FABulous ITALian Dinner PARTY

Laughing and gushing + FLIRTING
FAmily — children — BOYS I Adore.
MARC, trathen, Jason
and a call from Alex — tumbling HOME to Him
Late sleeping KISSES.
It BEGAN AGAIN WITH US.

Then this year, with
(THIS) Spilling Open arriving
in BOXes + BOXes
OH MY GOD! it's real
it's gonna go into THIS Big Wor
I learned more about myself this year
than ever Before
I know How HARD I can BE ON MYSELF
But I also know How STRONG.

· teach WOMEN's class
· work on PAINTings FOR Solo Show
· get Back into the darkroom — making my photos.
· go to Mills college ??
· Travel to N.Y.C.
· MOVE

THings I can do THIS year. @ 24.

sea

WHere IS HOME?

ABraAs
24 South
+ Luck
acing.

11pm

* TOP OF THE MARK HOPKINS HOTEL.

ON MY OWN.

Listening to Lavay + her Band

Swing ———————→ DANCING

till I'M sweating!

——————— ON MY OWN!

A Perfect SanFrancisco

Night.

THE SKY IS OPEN.

I've gotten excited to move. I want

A BIG room where I can have

PAINT everywhere ~ music on

and BOOKS everywhere

in Between.

~ MAKE · A · PLAN ~

light

REMEMBER to
STAY OUT
OF YOUR
OWN
way, and
what is
yours will
come
to you.

this Regunter

HOW it...
It Goes

afternoons
remembered

Holdin

THE PERSIMMON
I Tied to MY WI
WITH
Blue
string
is now ripe.

THIS Way aria was

BE TWIXT and BETWEEN

colors of noms

getting ready for my first on my own

Francis Mill and James Short SHOW!

has invited me to show in their

GALLery on Sutter st. in downTOWN

SAN FRANCISCO. it will run for 6 weeks
in April.

BETWIXT and BEWEEN is going to be THE SHOW'S Title. → THOSE
words describe these growing times so well.
THE CONTRADICTIONS challenges and in
between MESS of this life we are making.

* Can there Be Beauty in the tangles?

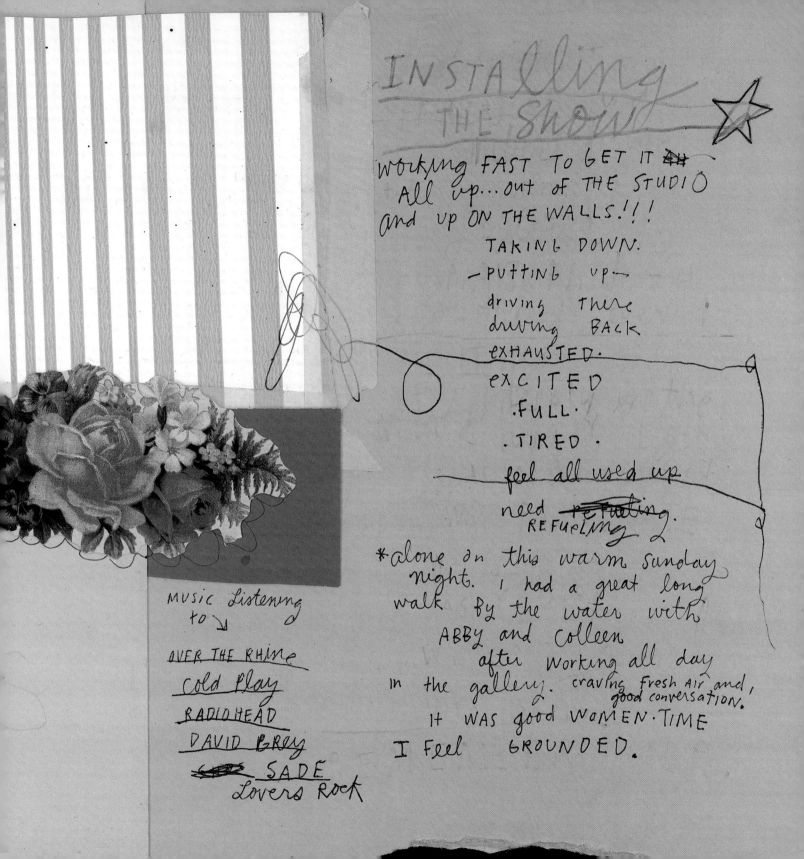

INSTALLING THE SHOW

WORKING FAST TO GET IT ~~ALL~~
All up...out of THE STUDIO
and up ON THE WALLS.!!!

TAKING DOWN.
-PUTTING up-
driving there
driving BACK
EXHAUSTED.

EXCITED
.FULL.
.TIRED.

feel all used up

need ~~refueling~~.
REFUELING

*alone on this warm sunday
night. i had a great long
walk by the water with
ABBY and Colleen
after working all day
in the gallery. craving fresh air and,
good conversation.
it was good WOMEN·TIME
I feel GROUNDED.

MUSIC Listening
to ↓

OVER THE RHINE
Cold Play
RADIOHEAD
DAVID GREY
SADE
Lovers Rock

I feel pressure to make
this show so good!
so strong! so amazing!
there is little room
for ..."just a first try"

leap.

It is the night of the Big Art opening. (I am wearing my Italian long skirt to remind me of that strength.) I can get so nervous about the art scene around here. what is # it? — the flashy clothes and coolness level? I want to connect to the women at these openings, not get myself all spun out with comparing myself and feeling so retarded and NERVOUS.

...ut Tonight I feel BETTER. I felt
all of us making our way in
this big and tiny world.
     The swirling of compliments
felt good ~ but left me with
thoughts of wanting to know more
of what the other WOMEN
                              I was meeting
do. WHAt their # stories are.
     I TRied $ to just
close my eyes and feel
this experience. (DAD always reminds
                              me to do THIS...)
"close your eyes + listen to the words."

Tonight was completely the
epitomy of what I feared
and craved of the
ART World.
      I like the good
   real folks I met tonight.
      sincere. good women. kind guys.
Lots of talking and real connection.
$ I am reminded of that line —
   If you don't go
      You don't
         see
   I feel I faced my intimidation
   tonight of this scene.
      just showed up for it —
      AND MADE IT. and

sometimes I feel all of this
RUShing and swirling
spinning in my BODY
and Nothing can seep in.
it JUST SWIRLS By
my eyes
——— feel this ———
Being this Age feels insane
at times.
So much "BECOMING" and
Vast OPEN changing
I want to stop All of this preparing FOR
STOP AND JUST feel this morning.
I feel THICK too and I dont Like
Judging my BODY.
I want to USE it FOR exploring + dancing
AND LIVING. I dont want to stare
Silently at its issues — But I DO + It's human
COVER — SHOW — Cover·SHOW — cover.
IT is amazing — all that I do to myself
to try to Bring peace to THE BODY I HAVE.

what
is
Left over.

sometimes
I feel thrilled
at this second
chance for SPILLING OPEN
to Be released again
to go FARther into the
world + into Needed ArMs.
(other times It MAKes me
overwhelmed to think of
all THIS opening up.)
CHANGE is always
Waiting around the
corners of our lives.
Is thAt HOW Life is revealed to us?
THE unexpected Left
TurNs?
and the FAITH IN the TURN...

I always find myself
living in moments
between going HOME...

windows of time

arriving HOME

leaving HOME

heading
HOME.

home keeps shifting

christMAS ROAD TRIP HOME

The sun on my shoulders
as I sit at Jlama Beach just
above SANTA BARBARA, where I am
CAMping with Alex's family for THE
night. DUSK is setting iN.
the shadows Lengthen in THE
Late winter Light.
PEOPLe stretch and cartwheel,
CHILDren Build worlds in the SAND,
AND Parents reach to their
toES. When did I Last
Watch THE sun SET?

mom at my age.

WAS it
in
ITAly
on THE
Amalfi
COASt?

*evening
WALK

MY LAST
night in
ITAly—
eating
dinner
in the cafe
WHile
MEN
gathered
40
watch
on the THE BIG Soccer game
T.V.

TOMATO MoZZAReLLa BASil SandwiCH
in glee → And took an extra one
with me For the long TRIP HOME.

I ate my

I WANT to BE WITH MY FAMILY.
after Finishing Anne Lamott's
TRAVELING MERCIES I swell with emotion
FOR the RIGHT HERE TIMES Together.
HUMBLE + HUMAN. not just getting "THE
up-dates" on EACHOTHER — experiencing
Something new together.
Anne Lamott writes a lot about her dad,
WHO WAS A WRITER Like MY DAD. I
just don't want to miss my Life with them
Because I'm too Busy ——→ going HOME
tomorrow will Be good!
 ·dancing with Anna.
 celebrating Mom.
~Listening talking about→Projects with DAD.
 to THE WORDS

BIG MOON Walk WITH DAD → remembering the
RIGHT HERE TIMES under THE STARS camping
together Just up TALKING and
STORY telling

BIG WIDE MOON UP there

DAD's Stories.

SI VOUS POSSEDEZ
Participez à la Loto Soleil
des viandes Maple Leaf!

remembering putting
toothPASTE ON MY MOSQUITO BITES (He SAID
It would make 'em stop Itching)

★ DAD making a little MOVI
in N.Y.C in the 70's.

We want these answers.
These solutions.
WE TRY so hard. WE Wait.

Big IT is a mixture of dreaming
and FAR and then turning
TOWARDS what is just right here.
right now.
Look at ALL we have saved so
FAR as proof! proof we are
KNOWN. proof we are Loved.
somehow seen.

everything I need. everything I craved. everything
isnt the answer

I feel I TAKE on Life Like
A PROJECT most OF THE TIME. I work
hard to "FINISH MYSELF up" SO
OTHERS get me all "complete and clean"
But I forget to leave room FOR
MYSelf to feel TANGLED. and
UNmade. But you see,

I am feeling these DAYs like
THOSE TANGLED PARTS ⟶ ARE THE
MOST interesting PARTS.
These are the Bits I want
to KNOW ABOUT in Others.

✳ Like today, weeding in the sun
picking clovers FROM the funny
FRONT GARDEN I have MADe
Blabbing on the phone with
my Little sister ANNA ⟶ with those
WHITE ol' legs of Mine peeking OUT
OF MY wrinkled Black skirt,
HAIR PINNED BACK   V8 JUICE

Sitting on the sidewalk in a
Little afternoon in my Life.

I AM NOT A ~~FINISH~~
✳   FINISHed PRODUCT

Maybe it comes full circle.
I look At what I feared in ME, what I can
PUSH so FAR AWAY FROM ⟶ Today I
am willing to see this happening, to
HOLD THESE contradictions
~ 24 and there is so much more ~

THANK YOU ALL SO VERY MUCH

* THE wonderful Friendships in my Life. THANKS

Megan RoBerts, Tymaree Cook, Jason Peacock, Megan Brown, Laurie Wagner, Jen Walsh, HadleyWalsh, Amelia and Russ, Rebecca Tourino, Natalie cuss, Leigh Kellis, Helena Simon, Zoe Wagner, Meagan Denroff, Jaysie castro, molly Franks, Marc Albert, Brian Heller, Aaron Renton, Brandt Browne, Robbie and DebBie, Elise Kohl brant, Hannah Finnie, Laura Sechi, Amanda Hughes, Yvathen Heckman, Chris Johnson, Juice, Karen MeAliffe, Amanda Mandalia, Zamer+Anna Nelson, DArBARA+chuck osburn, Michelle Potter (and ERiN O), Toni Pezone, Cynthia + Nari Richards, Steve Routt, SiouxZie Ruff, RuBy W, Nicki Smith, Lauren Chang, Elke Snyder, Jon SantoS, Medina Tung, Abby W____, Mark Wagner, Patrick SummAr, BikrAm YoGA (christy + cal), D____ Delpart, Ene+scott, Susi, Bill + Lauren Engl____ ____ in Funkle Mondays bi, Francis Mill, Jessica Parch, Eun-HA Pack, ____ Simmons, and also Grand pa. NANA

THE CARE and strength of these folks!

Becky Denenote, Jennifer Rudolf Walsh, Pamela Cannon, Dennis Love, Sally Marvin, Carol Schneider, Dan RemBert, Bruce Tracy and Ann Godoff Jay Mandel, Andrea Brewster, Eun-HA Pack, Misa

DAD → JOHN KENT HARRISON → YOU taught me to "FOLLOW THE ROAD LESS TRAVELED" and Listen to the Words With my eyes closed. THANK YOU FOR THE ADVENTURE, Brave on the rocks!

MOM - Lois WARD HARRISON — THANK YOU FOR YOUR grace And COLORS. YOU ARE AN Extraordinary MOTHER and I AM SO BLESSED.

ANNA KENT HARRISON YOU ARE FUNNY, YOU ARE WISE, you GOT STYLE, YOU ARE SEXY, YOU ARE STRONG, and I LOVE that you ARE MY SISTER!

SUSAN KENNEDY "THE PAGES ARE DONE" OH MY!! I respect AND Adore OUR wonderful FRIENDSHIP, especially all OF its FUNNY and BASIC Bits. I LOVE YOU.

Laurie Wagner and Family — HONEY, DARLin' THANK YOU! For riceFIGHTS and WINE Drinking on little CHAIRS in the kitchen. YOU ARE AN AMAZING and POWERFUL Voice. Your Writing RULES and Your LOVE GLOWS.

My BACK-UP FAMILY Laura, Steven, Lilli and Nicole. Thank You for Hot Baths, Perfect Drinks, COZY Snuggles, ~~AND~~ → AND the BIG LOVE and CARE.

HiLARY SWANK YOUR CRAFT and PASSION inspire ME to BE A BRAVER ARTIST. THANK YOU For reaching OUT to ME and SHARING FROM Your HEART. Bless You.

ALEXANDER KOPPS TOGETHER WE HAVE MADE A place in OUR Lives We Will HAVE ForEVER. I'll MEET YOU there. SAB.

For MORE information Visit: www.sabrinawardharrison.com

WRITERS: I THANK YOU For Your wisdom
BarbaraKingSolver, Anna Quindlen, Sue Bender, Natalie Goldberg, Rilke, Anne Lamott, Stephanie Dowrick, Lynn Franks, MAY SARTON, Pablo Neruda, Naomi Wolf, Mary Oliver, Jenny Read, Dave Eggers, Cheri Huber, Hugh Prather, Laurie Wagner, SARK, Adrienne Cunningham Blank, ReBecca TOURINO, DAN Price

☆ THANK You for the MusiC of ☆
ANi Difranco, Andrea Bocelli, Patsy Cline, Beastie Boys, David Grey, Lucinda Williams, Lauren Hill, Joan BaEz, BB King, Chet BAKER, Over the RINE, CAT POWER, Paolo Conte, Miles Davis, Cowboy Junkies, Sade, Tracy chapman,

1937
NANA